CASA di MIR MONTESSORI
ELEMENTARY SCHOOL

A Family in Morocco

LIBRARY OF CONGRESS CATALOGING-IN-PUBLICATION DATA

Stewart, Judy (Judy Diane)
  A family in Morocco.

  Originally published as: Moroccan family. 1985.
  Summary: Text and photographs present the life of
twelve-year-old Malika and her family, residents of
Tangier, Morocco.
  1. Morocco — Social life and customs — Juvenile
literature. [1. Morocco — Social life and customs]
I. Matthews, Jenny, ill. II. Title.
DT312.S84   1986   964'.05   86-54
ISBN 0-8225-1664-0 (lib. bdg.)

Manufactured in the United States of America

2 3 4 5 6 7 8 9 10 96 95 94 93 92 91 90 89 88 87

A Family in Morocco

Judy Stewart
Photographs by Jenny Matthews

Lerner Publications Company · Minneapolis

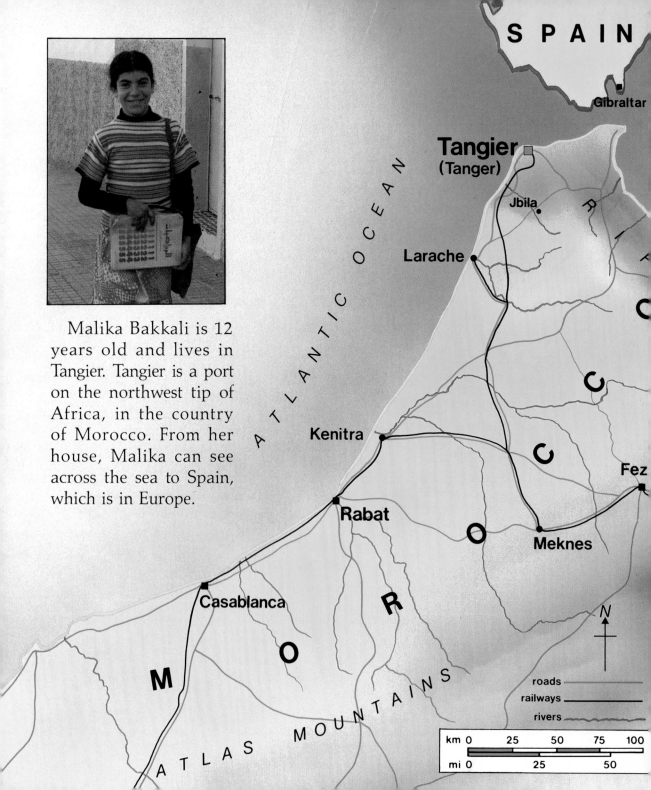

Malika Bakkali is 12 years old and lives in Tangier. Tangier is a port on the northwest tip of Africa, in the country of Morocco. From her house, Malika can see across the sea to Spain, which is in Europe.

SPAIN

Gibraltar

Tangier
(Tanger)

Jbila

Larache

R I F

ATLANTIC OCEAN

Kenitra

Fez

Rabat

O

Meknes

C

Casablanca

M

O

R

N

ATLAS MOUNTAINS

roads
railways
rivers

km 0   25   50   75   100

mi 0   25   50

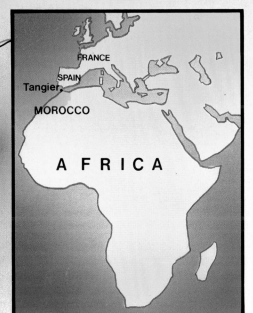

Malika has two brothers and four sisters. Her sister Fatima is 16, and the others are all younger than Malika. Her brothers are Mustafa and Karim, and two of her little sisters are Naima and Rashida. Their mother is carrying the baby, Aisha, on her back.

Malika's mother is wearing a *jellaba*, a long coat with a big hood. She is also wearing a veil over her face. Married ladies in Moroccan towns often cover their faces when they go out, because of modesty.

Malika's family's house has a kitchen and store-room downstairs and two rooms upstairs.

Malika likes to help her mother make bread. They have bread with every meal and use pieces of bread like spoons to scoop up their food. Malika's mother makes four big, round loaves of bread every day.

Making bread is hard work. Malika usually has to let her mother finish the kneading.

When Malika's mother cooks or does housework, she often carries Aisha on her back. Aisha never cries when she's carried like that.

Before school, Malika puts the bread on a wooden board, called a *wasala*, and carries it to the baker's oven in the next block. On the way, she meets her friends taking their bread to be baked. They race each other, trying not to drop the bread. The baker never gets the loaves mixed up in the oven, because each family stamps their own mark on them.

7

Malika's mother buys most of the family's food at the market. She shops nearly every day. In Tangier, the market is very noisy and crowded. Cars honk their horns, and men shout *"Balek! Balek!,"* which means "Look out!," as they push loaded carts through the crowds.

The shops and stalls sell almost everything. There are rows of butchers' shops, vegetable stalls, spice stalls, and many others. The market is full of different smells and colors.

On Thursdays and Sundays, people come from nearby villages to sell eggs and vegetables, and to buy what they need from town. The women wear big straw hats and striped skirts. Malika's mother prefers to buy from them because she knows the food is fresh.

Malika likes the orange stalls best. In winter and spring, her family eats oranges almost every day. They also put orange-flowers in their tea, and orange-flower water in their cakes and desserts.

Morocco is famous for its oranges. South of Tangier there are huge groves of orange trees. Truckloads of oranges are sent from Tangier by ship to Europe.

9

Malika's family speaks Arabic, like most people in Tangier. Some people from other parts of Morocco speak Berber.

At school, Malika is learning to read and write Arabic. You read Arabic from right to left. Malika's name, which means "Queen" in Arabic, looks like this:

ملكة بكالى   Malika Bakkali

Malika goes to the same school as Naima and Mustafa. They walk the short distance to school, but they go at different times. There aren't enough classrooms for all the classes to have school at the same time. This means someone's always home to help Malika's mother.

Malika is studying arithmetic, the history and geography of Morocco, French, and religion, as well as Arabic.

Malika has learned that Morocco was once a much bigger country. It even included northern Spain. That's why so many places in Spain have Arabic names. Later, the French and Spanish came to rule Morocco.

Many people in Tangier still speak French or Spanish, although Morocco became an independent country before Malika was born. Malika has been learning French for two years, but says she still isn't very good at it.

Morocco is a Muslim country, and in Malika's religion class they read the Koran. This is the Muslim holy book. She often has to learn parts of the Koran for homework. The garden is her favorite place to study, because she can read out loud without disturbing anyone.

After school, if there's nothing else to do, Malika can watch TV for a while. Because Tangier is so near Spain and Gibraltar, she can watch their TV programs too. Malika doesn't understand Spanish or English, so she only watches their cartoons.

Mustafa plays soccer with his friends after school. He only stops if there's soccer on TV.

Once a week, Malika goes to the *hamam*, or Turkish bath, with her sister Fatima. Each room in the steam bath is hotter and steamier than the last.

In the hottest room, there are faucets with hot water for washing. The water is heated by a wood-burning stove outside the baths. Malika and her sister spend a long time sitting in the hot, steamy rooms, soaping and shampooing and eating oranges. They end up very clean, but when they come out they have to be careful not to get cold.

Friday is a special day for Muslims, so there's no
school that day. This means the Bakkalis can have lunch
together. They usually have *couscous* on Fridays. Couscous
is made from flour rolled into tiny balls and steamed in
a special pan. It looks sort of like rice and tastes like
noodles. It's served with a meat and vegetable stew
on top.

Malika's family all eats from one big dish in the middle
of a low, round table.

Before and after the meal, a pan of water and some soap is passed around, and everyone washes their hands. Before they begin to eat they all say *"Bismillah,"* which means "in the name of God."

On Fridays, Malika's father goes to pray at the mosque. He leaves his shoes by the door of the mosque, just like he would at home. His wife usually prays at home.

Muslims are supposed to pray five times a day. A man calls from the top of each mosque to remind them when it's time to pray. People stop whatever they're doing, get out their prayer mats, and face Mecca. This is a town in Saudi Arabia which is a holy place for Muslims.

15

Malika's father is a weaver. His workshop is in a narrow street in the old part of town. It's close to the shops of a lot of other weavers.

Malika's father has two looms which he made himself. He can weave about 20 feet (6 meters) of cloth in a day. He sells it for about 50 *dirhams* a yard. In Tangier, a chicken costs 20 dirhams, and a liter of Coca-Cola (Malika's favorite drink) costs about 2 dirhams.

Sometimes Malika's father goes to the country to buy wool which is spun by the village women. Before he threads the wool onto the loom, he winds it onto a wooden frame to keep it from getting tangled.

Malika thinks her father makes beautiful woolen cloth. But more and more people prefer cloth made in textile factories. There are lots of these factories in Tangier and other big towns. The material from the factories isn't made of real wool and it doesn't last as long. But it's cheaper and more fashionable.

When Malika's father doesn't have much work to do, he goes to his favorite cafe to drink tea, talk to his friends, and watch the people passing by. The man next to him in this picture is wearing a jellaba made out of cloth woven by him.

Malika's father has lived in Tangier all his life, but her mother was born in a mountain village called Jbila. It's about 50 miles (80 kilometers) from Tangier. Sometimes the family goes there to visit Malika's uncle Mohamed and aunt Zakia.

To reach Jbila, they take the bus early in the morning. They have a long walk from the bus because there are no roads to Jbila. They have to cross a stream and then walk uphill for an hour.

On the way, they meet people going down the track from the village. Some are on mules or donkeys and some on foot. They always say hello and ask for news of Tangier.

Malika's family takes to Jbila presents of tea, sugar, oil, and candy for the children.

Uncle Mohamed's house is the first one in the village. Jbila has only 15 houses, and no stores, cafes or schools. But like every village in Morocco, Jbila has a place where the children learn to read the Koran.

Mohamed built his house with some help from his neighbors. It's made of home-made bricks, and the walls are whitewashed with lime. His family grows vegetables in a garden next to the house.

Mohamed also has one hectare (about two and a half acres) of land in the valley. Malika's cousin, Abdullah, plows it to get it ready for planting wheat and barley.

Malika loves visiting her relatives. Everyone gets up at dawn and there's always plenty to do. First, Aunt Zakia milks the goats and the cow. Then the goats are sent to join the village flocks. The milk is made into cheese, butter and buttermilk. The family also keeps chickens for eggs and meat.

As soon as they wake, Malika and her cousins Hafida and Aziza fetch water from the spring. Malika thinks the water tastes much better than in Tangier. She never realized how much water her family uses until she came to Jbila and had to carry it all in buckets.

Zakia makes even more bread than Malika's mother. She grinds wheat into flour on a grindstone in her neighbor's house. Then she makes the dough into round, flat loaves.

The bread is baked in a clay oven behind the house. Zakia gets a blazing fire going inside the oven. Then she puts it out and brushes away the ashes. She sprinkles the oven with water before putting in the bread. It doesn't take long to bake.

Every Tuesday, Malika's cousin Abdullah saddles up the mule and goes to the country market. It's half a day's journey away. Markets are named after the day of the week on which they're held. The market Abdullah goes to is called Souk El Tleta, or "Tuesday market."

Abdullah takes chickens and vegetables to sell. He wants to buy sandals, oranges, and kerosene for the lamps. If the family needed something special, he would normally sell a goat. But last year, a drought killed half the animals in the village.

Mohamed hasn't much land, so Abdullah might go to Tangier to look for a job. Many people leave their village to look for work in towns like Tangier or Casablanca. They usually go where they have relatives to help them. Abdullah would probably stay with Malika's family.

After three days in Jbila, it's time to go home. Zakia gives Mrs. Bakkali lots of vegetables, some freshly baked bread and two chickens to take back to Tangier.

Malika's family gets home in the afternoon. Malika's mother has a friend over for tea. She often has visitors in the afternoon for tea and cakes. Usually they are aunts or cousins or neighbors.

Moroccan tea is very sweet, almost like honey. It starts with a handful of green tea in the teapot. Malika's mother adds boiling water, lots of sugar, and a big bunch of mint. The tea is served in thin glasses. It's polite to drink at least three glasses of tea.

The sugar which Malika's mother uses for tea comes in a *qaleb*, or sugar loaf. Each loaf weighs five and a half pounds (two and a half kilos). Rashida carries a loaf almost as big as she is.

Malika's mother was given her silver teapot when she married. In Morocco, women are often given a tea set on their wedding day. This teapot came from Manchester, England.

Malika knows a lot about England because her uncle Salem lives there. He visits them in Tangier every summer. Someday he plans to come live in Tangier again. He already owns some land and is going to build a house.

Lots of tourists visit Tangier. They don't speak Arabic, but some of them speak French. They come to buy the beautiful things in the bazaars—silver tea sets, amber jewelry, leather bags, and wool carpets. Sometimes they look into Malika's father's shop and he offers them a glass of tea.

Tourists also visit Tangier because of the beach. In summer, Tangier's lovely sandy beach is crowded with tourists. People from other parts of Morocco, where it gets too hot, also vacation in Tangier. Because of the ocean breezes, Tangier rarely gets very hot.

In the spring, when it's too cool to swim, the beach isn't as crowded. Early in the morning, while the tourists are still eating breakfast in their hotels, the beach is almost empty. Only a few Moroccans and some camels that the tourists ride are out.

Sometimes Malika goes with her brothers and sisters to play on the beach. She's too shy to talk to the tourists, but Mustafa sometimes speaks to them in French and all his brothers and sisters giggle.

When she's older, Malika wants to go see the countries the tourists come from. She might visit her uncle Salem and be a tourist in England.

Islam: A Major World Religion

The official religion of Morocco is Islam. It is one of the world's largest religions. Most of its followers are in the Middle East, North Africa, Indochina, and parts of Europe.

Islam is the religion preached by the Prophet Muhammad about 600 years after Christ. Muhammad was an Arab who was born in Mecca, and Mecca is still very important to the Islamic religion. Muhammad preached that there was only one God (Allah) and that he, Muhammad, was God's messenger. People who believe Muhammad's teachings and practice Islam are called Muslims.

The Koran is the holy book of the Muslims. Muslims believe it to be the words of God Himself as spoken to Muhammad by an angel. Parts of the Koran resemble the Bible and the Talmud (the Jewish holy book).

Faith in Allah and in the Koran is one of the Five Pillars of Islam. The other Pillars are prayer, almsgiving (giving to charity), fasting, and pilgrimage. Together they are the basis of Islam. Muslims must pray five times each day, facing Mecca. They must give to the poor and other charities. During the month of Ramadan, they must not eat or drink anything from sunup to sundown. And they must visit Mecca at least once during their life.

All of the other rules for everyday life are also contained in the Koran. In some Islamic countries, the Koran is the law, and is enforced in the courts.

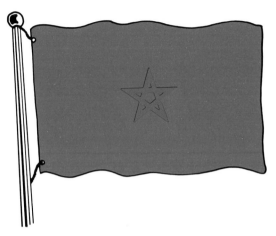

Facts about Morocco

Capital: Rabat

Language: Arabic
About one-third of Morocco's people speak a Berber dialect.

Form of Money: the dirham

Area: 177,177 square miles (458,730 square kilometers)
Morocco is a little larger in area than the state of Montana.

Population: about 24 million
The United States has about ten times as many people as Morocco.

EUROPE

ASIA

Morocco

AFRICA

AUSTRALIA

31

Families the World Over

Some children in foreign countries live like you do. Others live very differently. In these books, you can meet children from all over the world. You'll learn about their games and schools, their families and friends, and what it's like to grow up in a faraway land.

Lerner Publications Company
241 First Avenue North
Minneapolis, Minnesota 55401